Darcy

Thank you ...
for being a friend :)

Love your sista,
from another mista!

Maila

gratitude

COMPILED BY DAN ZADRA

DESIGNED BY STEVE POTTER

AND JENICA WILKIE

COMPENDIUM™
INCORPORATED

live inspired.

ACKNOWLEDGEMENTS

THESE QUOTATIONS WERE GATHERED LOVINGLY BUT UNSCIENTIFICALLY OVER SEVERAL YEARS AND/OR CONTRIBUTED BY MANY FRIENDS OR ACQUAINTANCES. SOME ARRIVED—AND SURVIVED IN OUR FILES—ON SCRAPS OF PAPER AND MAY THEREFORE BE IMPERFECTLY WORDED OR ATTRIBUTED. TO THE AUTHORS, CONTRIBUTORS AND ORIGINAL SOURCES, OUR THANKS, AND WHERE APPROPRIATE, OUR APOLOGIES.
—THE EDITORS

WITH SPECIAL THANKS TO

JASON ALDRICH, GERRY BAIRD, JAY BAIRD, NEIL BEATON, JOSIE BISSETT, LAURA BORO, M.H. CLARK, JIM AND ALYSSA DARRAGH & FAMILY, ROB ESTES, MICHAEL AND LEIANNE FLYNN & FAMILY, SARAH FORSTER, MICHAEL HEDGE, LIZ HEINLEIN, RENEE HOLMES, JENNIFER HURWITZ, HEIDI JONES, CAROL ANNE KENNEDY, JUNE MARTIN, JESSICA PHOENIX AND TOM DESLONGCHAMP, JANET POTTER & FAMILY, HEIDI & JOSÉ RODRIGUEZ, DIANE ROGER, ALIE SATTERLEE, KIRSTEN AND GARRETT SESSIONS, ANDREA SHIRLEY, HEIDI YAMADA & FAMILY, JUSTI AND TOTE YAMADA & FAMILY, BOB AND VAL YAMADA, KAZ AND KRISTIN YAMADA & FAMILY, TAI AND JOY YAMADA, ANNE ZADRA, AUGUST AND ARLINE ZADRA, AND GUS AND ROSIE ZADRA.

CREDITS

COMPILED BY DAN ZADRA

DESIGNED BY STEVE POTTER & JENICA WILKIE

ISBN: 978-1-932319-16-3

8TH PRINTING

THERE IS ALWAYS A TIME FOR GRATITUDE AND NEW BEGINNINGS. J. ROBERT MOSKIN

THE PACE OF LIFE CAN MAKE US BLUR WHAT'S IMPORTANT. WE ARE ALL VERY BUSY, THAT'S FOR SURE. BUT SOMEHOW WE MUST ALWAYS MAKE TIME FOR GRATITUDE AND NEW BEGINNINGS. THERE ARE MOMENTS IN LIFE WHEN YOU APPRECIATE SOMEONE SO MUCH THAT YOU JUST WANT TO STOP AND APPLAUD THEM. "FEELING GRATITUDE AND NOT EXPRESSING IT," SAID WILLIAM WARD, "IS LIKE WRAPPING A PRESENT AND NOT GIVING IT." IS THERE A TEACHER, LEADER OR MENTOR WHOSE WISDOM OR GUIDANCE MAY HAVE CHANGED THE TRAJECTORY OF YOUR LIFE? IS THERE A CUSTOMER WHO BELIEVED IN YOU, A COLLEAGUE WHO STOOD WITH YOU, A VOLUNTEER WHO SERVED WITH YOU, AN EMPLOYEE WHO MOVED MOUNTAINS FOR YOU, OR A FRIEND WHO LAUGHED OR CRIED WITH YOU? SOMETIMES WE CAN'T EXPRESS EXACTLY HOW WE FEEL ABOUT THEM, BUT THERE'S ONE THING WE CAN DO: WE CAN STOP AND LET THEM KNOW THAT WE ARE GRATEFUL.

Dan Zadra

THANK YOU

for being in our world

THERE ARE PEOPLE WHOM ONE APPRECIATES IMMEDIATELY AND FOREVER. EVEN TO KNOW THEY ARE ALIVE IN THE WORLD IS QUITE ENOUGH. NANCY SPAIN

THANK YOU

for making a difference

IT'S NOT WHAT WE HAVE IN OUR LIFE,

BUT WHO WE HAVE IN OUR LIFE THAT

COUNTS. J.M. LAURENCE

THANK YOU

for your wisdom

EACH OF US CAN LOOK BACK UPON SOMEONE WHO MADE A GREAT DIFFERENCE IN OUR LIVES, SOMEONE WHOSE WISDOM OR SIMPLE ACTS OF CARING MADE AN IMPRESSION UPON US. IN ALL LIKELIHOOD, IT WAS SOMEONE WHO SOUGHT NO RECOGNITION FOR THEIR DEED, OTHER THAN THE JOY OF KNOWING THAT, BY THEIR HAND, ANOTHER'S LIFE HAD BEEN MADE BETTER.

STEPHEN M. WOLF

THANK YOU

for being so thoughtful

MY HEART GIVES THANKS FOR

EMPTY MOMENTS GIVEN TO DREAMS,

AND FOR THOUGHTFUL PEOPLE WHO

HELP THOSE DREAMS COME TRUE.

WILLIAM S. BRAITHWAITE

THANK YOU
for being there

THE PERSON WE ALL LOVE AND

APPRECIATE IS THE ONE WHO'S

COMING IN THE DOOR WHEN

EVERYBODY ELSE IS GOING OUT.

MASON CANON

THANK YOU

for seeing the silver lining

WE CAN ALWAYS DEPEND ON SOME PEOPLE TO MAKE THE BEST, INSTEAD OF THE WORST, OF WHATEVER HAPPENS.

SANDRA WILDE

THANK YOU

for caring

THE PEOPLE WHO MAKE A DIFFERENCE ARE

NOT THE ONES WITH THE CREDENTIALS,

BUT THE ONES WITH THE CONCERN.

MAX LUCADO

THANK YOU

for sharing your thoughts

YOU GAVE ME YOUR TIME, THE MOST

THOUGHTFUL GIFT OF ALL. DAN ZADRA

THANK YOU

for listening

I FELT IT SHELTER TO SPEAK TO YOU.

EMILY DICKINSON

THANK YOU

for your inspiration

I AM GRATEFUL FOR WHATEVER HELPS

MY SPIRIT GROW. FLORIDA CALLOWAY

THANK YOU

for your faith

THANKS FOR SHOWING ME THAT EVEN ON THE DARKEST, RAINIEST DAYS THE SUN IS STILL THERE, JUST BEHIND THE CLOUDS, WAITING TO SHINE AGAIN. LISA HARLOW

THANK YOU
for your talent

WHEN WE FIND SOMEONE WHO

SURPASSES US, BE THANKFUL THAT

SUCH GIFTS ARE IN OUR MIDST, A PUBLIC

BANQUET TO WHICH WE ARE ALL INVITED.

DALE E. TURNER

THANK YOU

for your wonderful work

MANY PEOPLE HESITATE TO PRAISE THE PEOPLE THEY WORK WITH, THINKING IT WOULD SEEM LIKE FLATTERY. BUT OTHERS KNOW WE ARE IN A SPIRAL OF HELPING, A CONTEST OF GIVING. DALE DAUTEN

THANK YOU

for your leadership

YOU HAVE DONE MORE THAN LEAD,

YOU HAVE INSPIRED. DAN ZADRA

THANK YOU
for your character

A HERO IS SOMEONE WE CAN ADMIRE WITHOUT APOLOGY. KITTY KELLEY

THANK YOU

for your spirit

THOSE WHO LIVE PASSIONATELY TEACH

US HOW TO LOVE. THOSE WHO LOVE

PASSIONATELY TEACH US HOW TO LIVE.

SARAH BAN BREATHNACH

THANK YOU

for your principles

NOTHING IS MORE BEAUTIFUL OR POWERFUL THAN AN INDIVIDUAL ACTING OUT OF HIS OR HER CONSCIENCE, THUS HELPING TO BRING THE COLLECTIVE CONSCIENCE TO LIFE. NORMAN COUSINS

THANK YOU

for showing the way

SOMETIMES OUR LIGHT GOES OUT

BUT IS BLOWN INTO FLAME BY ANOTHER

HUMAN BEING. EACH OF US OWES

DEEPEST THANKS TO THOSE WHO HAVE

REKINDLED THIS INNER LIGHT.

ALBERT SCHWEITZER

THANK YOU

for your warmth

IT WAS ONLY A SUNNY SMILE...BUT IT

SCATTERED THE NIGHT LIKE MORNING

LIGHT, AND MADE THE DAY WORTH LIVING.

UNKNOWN

THANK YOU

for your kindness

KIND WORDS ARE JEWELS THAT LIVE IN

THE HEART AND SOUL, AND REMAIN AS

BLESSED MEMORIES YEARS AFTER THEY

HAVE BEEN SPOKEN. MARVEA JOHNSON

THANK YOU

for your encouragement

TOO OFTEN WE UNDERESTIMATE THE POWER OF A TOUCH, A SMILE, A KIND WORD, A LISTENING EAR, AN HONEST COMPLIMENT, OR THE SMALLEST ACT OF CARING, ALL OF WHICH HAVE THE POTENTIAL TO TURN A LIFE AROUND.

LEO BUSCAGLIA

THANK YOU

for your honesty

FEW DELIGHTS CAN EQUAL THE MERE

PRESENCE OF ONE WHOM WE TRUST

UTTERLY. GEORGE MACDONALD

THANK YOU
for your helping hand

TREASURE THE ONE WHO THINKS OF YOU WHEN ALL OTHERS ARE THINKING OF THEMSELVES.

JAMES GUNN

THANK YOU

for reaching out

THE WORK OF YOUR HEART, THE WORK OF

TAKING TIME TO LISTEN, TO HELP, IS ALSO

YOUR GIFT TO THE WHOLE OF THE WORLD.

JACK KORNFIELD

THANK YOU
for your touch

THERE ARE THOSE WHOSE LIVES

AFFECT ALL OTHERS AROUND THEM.

QUIETLY TOUCHING ONE HEART,

WHO IN TURN, TOUCHES ANOTHER.

REACHING OUT TO ENDS FURTHER

THAN THEY WOULD EVER KNOW.

WILLIAM BRADFIELD

THANK YOU

for your support

IF I CAN COUNT ON YOU, AND YOU

CAN COUNT ON ME, JUST THINK

WHAT A WONDERFUL WORLD

THIS WILL BE. CHILDHOOD RHYME

THANK YOU

for hanging in there

A FRIEND WALKS IN WHEN THE WHOLE

WORLD WALKS OUT. WALTER WINCHELL

THANK YOU

for staying in touch

NO MATTER WHERE WE ARE, WE NEED

THOSE FRIENDS WHO TRUDGE ACROSS

FROM THEIR NEIGHBORHOODS TO OURS.

STEPHEN PETERS

THANK YOU

for giving

YOU'VE TOUCHED PEOPLE AND KNOWN IT.

YOU'VE TOUCHED PEOPLE AND NEVER

MAY KNOW IT. EITHER WAY, YOU HAVE

SOMETHING TO GIVE. IT IS IN GIVING TO

ONE ANOTHER THAT EACH OF OUR LIVES

BECOMES MEANINGFUL.

LAURA SCHLESSINGER

THANK YOU

for your example

THOSE WHO KNOW AND LOVE YOU

SHALL RISE TO YOUR EXAMPLE AND

BE INSPIRED. UNKNOWN

THANK YOU

for spreading joy

YOUR GREATEST PLEASURE IS THAT

WHICH REBOUNDS FROM HEARTS

THAT YOU HAVE MADE GLAD.

HENRY WARD BEECHER

THANK YOU

for your big heart

PEOPLE WHO DEAL WITH LIFE

GENEROUSLY AND LARGE-HEARTEDLY

GO ON MULTIPLYING RELATIONSHIPS

TO THE END. ARTHUR C. BENSON

THANK YOU

for all you've done

AND COULD I HAVE BUT

ONE WISH THIS YEAR,

THIS ONLY WOULD IT BE:

I'D LIKE TO BE THE SORT OF FRIEND

THAT YOU HAVE BEEN TO ME.

EDGAR GUEST

THANK YOU

for the memories

PEOPLE WILL FORGET WHAT YOU SAID,

AND PEOPLE WILL FORGET WHAT YOU DID,

BUT PEOPLE WILL NEVER FORGET HOW

YOU MADE THEM FEEL.

BONNIE JEAN WASMUND

THANK YOU

for being you

FOR ALL THAT HAS BEEN, THANKS.

FOR ALL THAT WILL BE, YES!

DAG HAMMERSKJÖLD